THE BRIDE OF CHRIST

THE BRIDE OF CHRIST

A Love Story Study Guide

Elizabeth Wolfe

XULON PRESS

Xulon Press
2301 Lucien Way #415
Maitland, FL 32751
407.339.4217
www.xulonpress.com

Printed in the United States of America.

ISBN-13: 978-1-6305-0664-3

TABLE OF CONTENTS

INTRODUCTION

A RATHER LONG WHILE AFTER PUBLICATION, I decided one day to again read my book, *The Bride of Christ; A Love Story*. As I was reading, the Holy Spirit began to speak to me about the much deeper meaning of its chapters. He began asking me the questions that are asked in this study and teaching me things that I had not realized when I was writing the book initially.

The Bride of Christ; A Love Story, is a narrative about a girl Deborah who meets and marries a man. J.C., who typifies Jesus in the story. She does not realize who he is, nor does she understand her role as his bride. At least until the arrival of his twin, H.S. who moves in to show Deborah how a Bride of Christ thinks and behaves.

The first thing H.S. taught ME as visited the Bride of Christ; A Love Story is that the book is indeed (as many have asked, and I denied) autobiographical. I believe each of us is Deborah in ways not considered in our first read-through of the book. Reading it again with this insight, I saw myself in a new, constructive way through each of the incidents discussed in the book. So, I asked the Holy Spirit to help me write a study guide that would not only give understanding of the intense love of Jesus as our Bridegroom, but also a guide to understand the depth of the relationship He desires to have with all of us.

It is my hope that, as you read and study the questions asked here, you will ask Holy Spirit to renew your mind to whatever He has for *you personally in each step*. Remember, *there are no wrong answers!* Whether you are studying in a group (which can give varied insights to heighten the thought process) or alone, it is my hope and belief that Holy Spirit will "enlarge your tents" (Isa. 54:2 NKJV) through this study.

Be certain to enter each session of study with prayer, asking the Holy Spirit to reveal His personal message to you of who He presently knows you to be. You are unique in Him, so if someone else in your group answers a question differently, *don't decide what He has said to you is wrong.* Be diligent to pursue *your answer*, and let others be glad in and pursue *their* answers. *There is no right or wrong here*—just an unveiling of "Christ *in you* the hope of glory" (Col. 1:27). It is not a contest, rather, it is a mystery. A mystery that the Holy Spirit in you has all the solutions needed for the revelation of your glory.

Enjoy the creation of your "newness"!

Chapter 1

DEBORAH

HERE, WE FIND DEBORAH ON HER WEDDING DAY.
She is excited and, at the same time, concerned
about the details of the day; the plans for which,
unlike most weddings, were not clear. Since most
of us don't particularly care for the unknown—
especially in regards to something important—
she was a bit anxious.

1. If you are married, do you remember the day
of your wedding?

2. Had you planned for a long time to make certain *every detail* was correct?

3. Which of the carefully planned scenarios
went awry?

4. Were your emotions turbulent, fearful, happy, or all of these?

Deborah, interestingly enough, reflected on her past life as opposed to the future ceremony. All of it seemed to culminate in the joy of remembering the moment when Susan, her best friend, introduced her to J.C. She said it seemed He was "all about her."

5. When you were first introduced to Jesus, did you immediately believe that Jesus was "all about you"?

6. What do you think it means to have Him be "all about you"? Refer to verse #2 in the back of text, and relate that verse to your personal concept of your relationship with Jesus.

Write your answer here:

_____

_____

_____

Many of us are like Deborah in that we want so badly to believe that Jesus is "the same yesterday, today and forever" (Heb. 13:8 KJV); however, our past has caused us to distrust people. Deborah's father was obviously not someone she could trust, and this was causing her problems with J.C.

7. What was Susan's solution for Deborah?

It is the answer we all need to hear in our hearts. The key to understanding forgiveness is this:

Forgiveness is not a feeling. Forgiveness is something we do because it pleases Father God. It is part of learning submission and trust. He always intends His requests for our welfare.

We begin to "reign in life" (Rom. 5:17 AMP) when we learn to *receive* His grace, which is both His favor that gives us the ability to live from the provision He provided for us, and from the gift of righteousness of righteousness He bought at the Cross and gave to us.

8. Why do you think that on page 19 H.S. is referred to as J.C.'s identical twin? Write answer.

So, when Deborah is marrying J.C., she drops the pins and then drops a huge "damn." Her reactions were shame, followed by fear of what J.C. would think. However, J.C.'s reaction was entirely opposite of what she expected, and He gave her some advice that we *all* need to follow.

9. What did He tell her to do?

10. What were Deborah's emotions following this revelation?

11. When she said the word damn, do you think Jesus smiled, or do you think He was upset? Explain your thoughts.

_____

_____

_____

_____

Chapter 2

THE DREAM

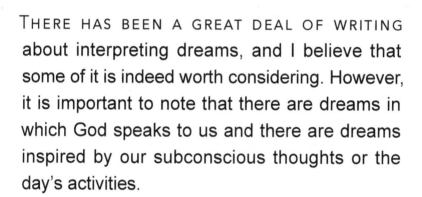

THERE HAS BEEN A GREAT DEAL OF WRITING about interpreting dreams, and I believe that some of it is indeed worth considering. However, it is important to note that there are dreams in which God speaks to us and there are dreams inspired by our subconscious thoughts or the day's activities.

Do you believe God has ever spoken to you in a dream? If so, write a brief summary of it.

_____

_____

_____

Consider the applications of the dream Deborah was having in terms of her life at the moment.

1. What are the spiritual implications of Deborah's order of lamb?

_____

_____

2. What does the word sustenance mean to us spiritually?

_____

_____

_____

3. Name some things that you think the other people in the dream could have been experiencing that made them unable to partake of the food immediately in front of them.

_____

_____

_____

4. What are you experiencing that is pre-
venting you from being able to see and
partake of your immediate blessings of
favor and love?

_____

_____

_____

If fear is one of the things you named as pre-
venting your progress, ask the Holy Spirit to
reveal its root to you and cause His Grace to
provide your escape by overcoming the fear or
by accepting and believing His love that "has no
fear" (1 John 4:18)!

In the sentences, both on page 24 and in the last
lines of the chapter, the references to dancing
around and to carrying on a loving-type of banter
with Jesus; does the idea of this type of conversation make you feel good, or do you question
being able to have this relationship with Him?
Consider this, and, if you choose, write your

feelings here. If in a group, it will help to hear others' feelings as well.

_____

_____

_____

Chapter 3

THE CEREMONY

IN THE FIRST PARAGRAPH OF THIS CHAPTER, Deborah states that her first thought was that Jesus had failed to "honor His Word to her."

1. Have you ever felt that Jesus failed to honor His Word to you? If so, it is perfectly acceptable to admit this. Jesus probably *already knew* your thoughts, right?

_____

_____

2. Does the thought of calling yourself Mrs. J.C. arouse any emotions in you? Note those here.

_____

If only we could all learn to reason with our problems as rationally as Susan did when she answered Deborah's anxious thoughts and what-ifs. Jesus, our Bridegroom, wants to bring us joy in every moment we are here on earth.

3. What are some times recently that you have worried about what others thought of you? What were the effects of these incidents on you?

_____

_____

Deborah was so thankful for Susan's "confident air to help calm her butterflies," but only Jesus can give us "confidence in the day of judgment" of ourselves and our situations (1 John 4:17b).

4. Look up this verse, and connect it to the paragraph above. What do you think the "day of judgment" is? Answer this here, and discuss if in a group.

_____

_____

_____

5. On page 29, J.C. responds to Deborah's inner image of herself by gently asking her to change her dress from off-white to white. Can you apply this to your own self-image?

_____

_____

_____

Read verse 17 in the back of the book.

6. What do you think is the difference between being "ceremonially clean" and "whiter than snow"? Does this relate in any way to being judged by people and, perhaps more importantly, by yourself?

_____

_____

_____

In 1 John 5:17 (AMP), we find the statement, "Because as He is, so are we in this world." In another verse, the Holy Spirit through Paul says, "There is therefore NOW no condemnation (no judging guilty of wrong) to those who are in Christ Jesus" (Rom. 8:1 AMP).

7. Do you think one meaning for the above verses could be, "there is no condemnation to those who possess in their hearts **His image** of who **they really are**"? Consider this in situations in your daily life. Write your answer here and discuss if in a group.

_____

_____

8. Deborah's fear was that she would be a disappointment to Jesus. Is that a ridiculous thought?

_____

_____

9. If you either agree or disagree with that question; explain your reasoning by finding scriptures

to confirm your thoughts. Write the references here and compare them to the 1 John and the Romans 8 references. Even if you only find one scripture, remind yourself frequently of *how He sees you*. It will cause you to feel "accepted in the Beloved" (Eph. 1:6 NKJV)—and that's a *good thing*!

_____

_____

_____

Finally, they reach the wedding site. Jesus opens the door and embraces Deborah. Notice on page 31 how Jesus only answers her questions about her inadequacies with praise. On page 32, it happens again when the joy she feels could not be quenched by any anxiety. Instead, her response to Father, Son, and Holy Spirit is uproarious laughter!

There is no way to find the peace and joy of the presence of God other than time spent *in His presence*! We often approach time with Him as a certain performance, i.e. praying, reading the Bible, reading a book, journaling, meeting with friends, etc. All of these are great things, but God is a "still small voice," (1 Kings 19:12 NKJV) and the need to try to please Him interferes with getting beyond the "veil" of our own ideas and into His realm of thought. It is there that He tells us He is *always* with us and pleased.

10. What are your feelings about that statement? Connect it with Jesus's remark about being non-traditional on page 33 and with the scripture and answers about the Scribes and Pharisees.

_____

_____

_____

Turn to the back of your book and read scriptures #22 and #23.

11. What do you think these verses mean in relation to what was just discussed concerning Jesus's feelings about your worth?

_____

_____

_____

If Jesus "believes the best of everyone in *all* situations," how could He ever be disappointed in us?

If God **accepted us** on the basis of **what Jesus did,** how could He be disappointed in us? God knew us before the foundation of the world—all our action and thoughts. Jesus took those onto **Himself** at the cross. Can there be any disappointment in love that is *constant*?

Read the last paragraph on page 34, and remember, it is only in hearing our God—heart—that we can begin to hear the music of His love and come to know who we *really are* in Him, *as* Him (1 John 4:17 KJV).

_____

_____

_____

Chapter 4

SHOPPING WHIRL

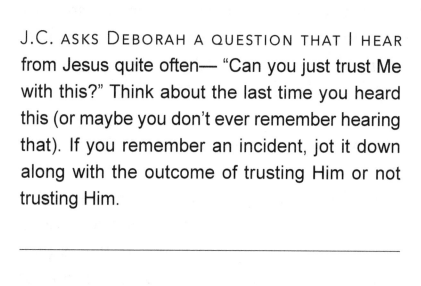

J.C. ASKS DEBORAH A QUESTION THAT I HEAR from Jesus quite often— "Can you just trust Me with this?" Think about the last time you heard this (or maybe you don't ever remember hearing that). If you remember an incident, jot it down along with the outcome of trusting Him or not trusting Him.

_____

_____

_____

Why do I ask you to write things down? I do so, because it helps to remember details of the things you note here. Hopefully, you will come back to your notes at some point in time and realize how much you have grown in those kinds of situations. I often go back after a few years and read my journals and am able to see where I have improved or still need to improve.

Becoming the bride of J.C. immediately presented Deborah with many new situations. One of which was knowing how to clothe herself as a joint heir in His kingdom. On page 37, we see her going from insecure, to indignant and shouting, to unfamiliar, nervous, and whispering.

Do you have any ideas on why J.C. takes her to the Faith store first and why the attendant's name is Hope? In the Hebrews, we find answers to this question. It says, "Now Faith is the assurance, the confirmation, the title deed, of things (we) **hope** for, being the proof of things (we) do **not see** and the **conviction** of their **reality**. (Faith perceiving as **real fact** what is not (yet) revealed to the **senses**.)" (Heb. 11:1) AMP.

1. What are your ideas concerning this scripture? Try looking up the definition of at least *some* of

these words if not *all* of them, then read it again using another definition of them. I made a list. For instance: assurance=security. Now read the verse again, using security instead of assurance. It often helps to make things easier to understand.

_____

_____

_____

Read in the last part of the page 37 paragraph, where Deborah is to be shown many "Faith-Outfits."

2. Find some scriptures about faith that will help clothe *you* beautifully. Write them here.

_____

_____

_____

3. Explain how these scriptures help you understand J.C.'s always being joyful.

_____

_____

_____

In Chapter 1, we learned that forgiveness is *not* a feeling. It is a *choice* which becomes a feeling. Here, we need to understand something about *joy*. **Joy is a feeling**. It is a feeling that lives in us as a characteristic of the Holy Spirit. Feeling joyful in "whatever we are doing at the moment" is a gift to us from Jesus that the Holy Spirit develops fully as we learn more about how to trust our days and circumstances to His leading. In order to be *led*, we have to hear the directions given in each situation. In order to do this, we must **practice three things: listening for, expecting to hear, and obeying what we hear.**

Notice the first bold word above—practice. **We do not learn to hear the voice of God by waiting until we are in a crisis situation to start spending time listening! The art of listening begins first in the natural realm.**

Do you listen to your children, your husband, your parents, and your co-workers? **Start practicing**

there, and then move on to **practicing** listening for Holy Spirit's voice when someone is talking to you. **Practice** not thinking about what you are going to say when they stop talking, nor while they are still speaking. My suggestion is to quietly ask the Holy Spirit to help you hear *their heart*. Often, they are struggling, and what they are saying is not really their heart's message. As soon as you can hear **their heart's real message, you can hear the Holy Spirit's solution!** Then, either speak what He says, or, if you hear nothing, **practice saying nothing.** Simply pray and ask to hear what you should say, or ask Him to give *them* the answer. Notice again the word *practice*. This is a learning experience of great value in not only your life and the lives of those close to you, but in strangers' lives as well.

Other than the three main categories, there are six things above that you are asked to practice.

4. List them here, and study them carefully.

_____

_____

_____

_____

_____

_____

You could make a 3x5 card with these (six or nine) things on it to carry along for situations you encounter.

Let me tell you something that happened in my life recently. A dear friend had a visitor in her home who she was trying, with God's help, to encourage and help develop a different identity model. One day, when I dropped by to encourage her, she was at a particularly low point in her circumstance. Because she had this young person in her home, she had many relational problems with others. She was broken-hearted. We prayed together, and I will confess that the solution I suggested did *not* come from the Holy Spirit. It came from my own hurt for my friend's circumstances.

Later in the evening, as I prayed and listened for the Holy Spirit's voice, I heard what I believe was the heart of the person making so many problems for my friend. She had an alcoholic father, married an addict, divorced him, finally married my friend's son, and for years had experienced the joys of a more normal, loving family than she possibly had ever known—she felt safe. But, a reminder of her past hurts and traumas made them resurface. She wasn't lashing out at my friend, rather she was expressing her *own fears*. Her heart was saying, *Oh no, I just can't go back to the hurt and the trauma of my past. This may break up my perfect family. I've got to stop this.*

Now, that I was no longer *judging her* (or me), I was able to pray very differently about all of it as I didn't see her as vicious, but as a victim of her own heart's need for the comfort and healing that would enable her to be part of the solution rather than an additional problem for my friend's family.

Look at J.C.'s reaction to Deborah when she appeared in the dress. He did not start thinking, *Well, here she goes again, not trusting what I know is best.* He became very interested in having her learn to "love it."

This is how we need to come to understand the nature of Jesus. **He did a cruel, undeserved death, so we could have a wonderful, victorious life; a life we can love!** We just need to trust Him that when we don't like what is happening, we need to look at our and others' **heart** issues. He has a promise and a plan to make it right for *everyone concerned.*

"God will continually revitalize you, implanting within you the passion to do what pleases Him" (Phil. 2:13 Passion Trans.) "[So] Do all things without grumbling and faultfinding, and complaining [against God] and questioning and doubting [among yourselves]" (Phil. 2:12-14 AMPC).

That passage describes the clothing Jesus bought for us. Some days they will fit more comfortably than others, but read this promise for your daily "work out" and put on the clothing that will reveal the *real you* and *your destiny.*

I heard Bishop T. D. Jakes say, "The seed holds the mystery of the tree and the tree holds the whole orchard." In each of us, there is a seed of destiny. We either cultivate it until the orchard comes forth, or we let it be choked by the thorns of life.

"Your Father [God] knows what you need before you ask Him" (Matt. 6:8). Some translations preface that verse with, "Don't you know?" Perhaps that is the most important thing—*we need to know* that our Father cares about us and knows what we need and hears the longings of our heart in the night when we are afraid and lonely and hungry and abused. He has made a way through and out of everything we are presently experiencing. Begin to seek wisdom and courage to hear and trust and obey the thing that the Father has planned for your path to victory and on to something that you will *love*.

An important step in this is to **visualize** yourself as you hear **God say** who you are—not as you may presently appear to be. If you have watched the Olympics, you may have noticed the skaters, **before they perform**, do turns and balance with a leg in the air and arms up. Why are they doing this? They are setting their goals and intentions in their minds and muscles, so only that is what they see and perform when they get on the ice. **Visualize your destiny, so that when you are on life's slick surfaces, you perform as a God-person!**

In the remainder of the chapter, J.C. teaches Deborah the behavior needed to become the bride she is destined to be. He shows her how to:

1. Praise in the midst of uncertainty.

2. Feel His mercy around her even when she doesn't understand exactly what is going on and to *expect* His mercy to prevail in all circumstances.

3. See the value of having humility in our destinies. (Deborah didn't like it either.)

4. Minister to those less fortunate, even when it is uncomfortable and possibly unpopular.

These are all areas of Christ's destiny in us—*as us*—in a world where we must learn to live where we are often hated for our belief and our visualization of our destiny in God. Jesus said, "I have given them your word and the world hated them because they are not of this world, even as I am not of this world" (John 17:14 NKJV). We must let the Holy Spirit teach us how to grow as the seed of the Word is planted in soil that is often not receptive to His seed.

Chapter 5

OFF TO DINNER

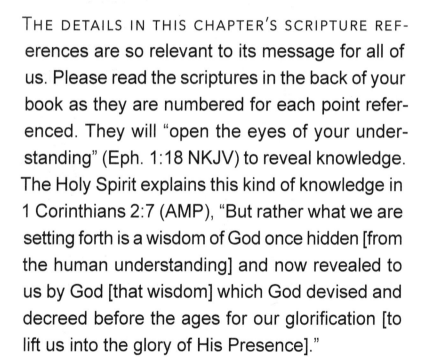

THE DETAILS IN THIS CHAPTER'S SCRIPTURE REF-
erences are so relevant to its message for all of
us. Please read the scriptures in the back of your
book as they are numbered for each point refer-
enced. They will "open the eyes of your understanding" (Eph. 1:18 NKJV) to reveal knowledge.
The Holy Spirit explains this kind of knowledge in
1 Corinthians 2:7 (AMP), "But rather what we are
setting forth is a wisdom of God once hidden [from
the human understanding] and now revealed to
us by God [that wisdom] which God devised and
decreed before the ages for our glorification [to
lift us into the glory of His Presence]."

Why did God reveal it *now*? He did so for *our* glorification! In John 17:22-23, Jesus says He has

given us the glory and honor which the Father gave to Him, so that we may be one even as He and Father and Holy Spirit are one. He wants us to be "as He is in this world" (1 John 4:17). It's time for us to quit waiting to **go somewhere** in order to be redeemed. Redemption is **a now thing in Christ Jesus.**

1. In John 17:23, for what three purposes did Jesus ask His Father to give us His same measure of glory and honor? Answer below and explain what you think this means. Then, relate this to your life at present.

_____

_____

_____

On page 52, Deborah says that J.C. must be the P.R. person for His Dad.

2. Using the scriptures in the back of the book, (#39, #40, and #41) tell what J.C. told her His title means. Translate this into your personal life.

Write your answers below. Commit to memory this promise of who you are in Him.

_____

_____

_____

David said, "He has prepared a table before me in the presence of my enemies" (Ps. 23:5 NIV). At the top of page 54, J.C. makes a very important statement of truth about the value of having a relationship with Him.

3. How does this statement relate to marriage and all other realms of relationship in our world? Answer here.

_____

_____

_____

On page 55, Deborah makes a statement about two different tones of voice. If we learn to think this way about hearing the **Lord's quiet voice** versus hearing condemnation, anxiety, and fear, we will make great progress toward always hearing His directions to the path of life.

Most of us are still learning to differentiate between these voices. This is especially difficult if in our childhood we were controlled by criticism and corrected by abuse. If this is the case, it is hard *not* to believe Jesus corrects and directs in the same critical, abusive way to which we may be accustomed. Learning to believe the truth about Jesus's ways of thinking and speaking involves both a decision to **hear** His voice and also to **practice listening for Him**, but this practice is such a valuable, profitable way in which to live our best lives.

As you go through this chapter and all of the chapters, notice one very important thing—*Jesus does not try to **fix** Deborah!* He just **loves** her no matter how difficult she becomes. *How many relationships would be saved if we would/could realize that we cannot **fix** another person? That is God's job.* Our job is to learn to **love** them. We *do not* have to agree with them! Notice at the bottom of page 55 how J.C. does not try to talk her out of the dish she chose. He simply said, "That is fine with me. We will call the waiter." Then, He quietly went about doing what He knew was best for **Him.** Again, at the bottom of page 56, notice His response to her next choice and what He replied to her. How are you at *freeing* those with whom you are in relationship? How are you at trying to *fix* those with whom you are in relationship?

Keep in mind that J.C. told Deborah *He* is in charge of personal relationships—that includes ours.

4. What would understanding J.C.'s actions and intentions mean to your relationships—husband/wife, parents, children, job, friends, church leaders, etc.? Note your thoughts here, and, if you choose, list each relationship and make notes as to how you can contribute to freedom in each. At the end of the exercise, you may want to change your thought processes.

_____

_____

_____

On page 57, J.C. describes what happens when we try to **fix** everyone and every situation. Notice that He never used the word **you** in His explanation of why the choices she was making were bad for her. He simply referred to the problems **the dishes** had—not to **her choices**. Now, look at the third paragraph, read aloud what He told her is the result of always needing to fix everyone and everything. Write that here.

_____

_____

_____

Then, if you choose, relate this to your own relationships and write your answers here.

_____

_____

_____

On page 57, the ingredients for *nourishing life-relationships* are found. List them here. There are also Scripture references for each of the ingredients listed. You might enjoy and be uplifted by finding them and writing the references beside the word for future or current use.

_____

_____

_____

_____

_____

Chapter 6

HIS GIFTS

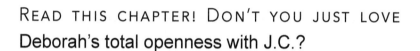

READ THIS CHAPTER! DON'T YOU JUST LOVE Deborah's total openness with J.C.?

Check your feelings about her responses to what He is saying to her. I am often as bewildered as she is about understanding my role in God's kingdom. The truth is that we try to make our gifts mortal, and they are truly **immortal**.

Jesus gives us **His** Name, i.e. **His** Nature. He is the **great I AM,** and we are given the **inherent opportunity** to be **like Him**. We often we get confused because we can neither "**be-have**" **nor** "**be-lieve**" the way He does. **This is because what Jesus is offering us is a** *relationship— not a job.*

The definition for relationship is: "The way in which two or more are connected by blood, marriage, or community and **how they *relate* to and *regard each* <u>other</u>"**.[1]

God's assurance to us in John 1:12-13 is that we are His own children. **We are born again into a new bloodline by the Blood of Jesus.** This requires a serious, personal identity change—a change which takes time and prayer and studying Jesus's life in order to understand who **we really are** and how to relate to situations **as that person**.

J.C. is trying to give Deborah (and *us*) a new identity of our **unlimited self.**

Notice how, at the bottom of page 60, J.C. does not agree or disagree with her response. Instead, He presents her with a different way of seeing herself—a way that says something positive.

1. Which of His P.R. skills (book, page 52) does J.C. use in this lesson for Deborah?

Notice what wonderful communication skills are exhibited by J.C. on pages 60-61.

2. At the bottom of page 61, what happens? Deborah begins to gradually get the picture for herself.

It is so important to read the scriptures provided as reference on these pages and make notes of the characteristics J.C. presents of His nature.

3. Make these notes here, and, more importantly, **note that this is who your unlimited self really is.** Note these here in first person. *Lay claim to your inheritance!* If in a group, please encourage discussion of this.

———————————————————

———————————————————

———————————————————

At the bottom of page 62, J.C. gives Deborah some incentive to **find** (not only read about) her real self. She calls them "job perks," and He laughs and tells her these benefits are more beneficial and lasting. *Notice, Deborah has yet to catch the relationship idea—she is still in the **job mode.***

4. See #58 scripture. List the promises of this verse and note they are to glorify the Father.

_____

_____

_____

J.C. keeps answering all Deborah's doubts with encouragement and gives her the pattern for learning to **reign** as His Bride **(as opposed to struggling to *perform*)**! He explains that, *yes, she will be tested*, but she cannot fail **if** she keeps her mind on the goal of being her **unlimited self!**

Learn to feel what she says in the center of page 65 about how He makes her feel even though she is not always that person as of yet. The last sentence on page 65 says voumes about who we are to Jesus. All *He* wants to be *for* us and has *bought and paid for us to have* is in the sentence at the center of page 66. We can be excited that we have a **whole lifetime of gifts to open and learn to use.** Read scripture #65—it's so yummy!

Go to the bottom of page 66, and read what J.C. considered the most valuable gift he could give Deborah. Continue reading about the gifts and characteristics of the Holy Spirit. J.C. said the Holy Spirit is our **personal trainer.** In other words, **He will "train" each of us according to our own personal destiny and help "lift the weights" for us.** It is when we start comparing ourselves among ourselves that we lose track of **our trainer's goals.**

5. For instance, suppose you are invited to a gathering at a home or club where you have never been, and so you have no idea what to expect concerning location, dress, guest list, etc. How would you feel? Would your first thoughts be, *Oh, this is going to be exciting and fun?* Or, would you think, *Oh no! I have no idea what to wear. I'm going to call Ann and see what she is wearing?* What happens when you call Ann and discover her dress sounds prettier or more

appropriate than yours? Write your thoughts here. Discuss if in a group.

_____

_____

_____

Read on page 62 when she compares herself to an *imaginary person* and decided she could never be good enough.

This same "less-than enough" approach to our everyday life and to becoming all that we were created to be keeps us stuck in the "lesser places"!

Now look at the bottom of page 63 at J.C.'s response to Deborah's reactions, and realize that all the comparison times come to give you an *opportunity* to learn who you **really are. Everything in life with Jesus is an opportunity!**

6. Make a note of, on page 64, what they were enjoying most, and reflect on that in terms of your relationship with Jesus.

7. Make a note here of some of the Holy Spirit's gifts with which J.C. promises Deborah will be filled.

_____

_____

_____

8. From the top of page 68, make a reference here of what J.C. says is one of the Holy Spirit's best "subjects."

_____

_____

_____

9. Write the needs in your life which would cause you to "sign up" for the Holy Spirit's 101 class in overcoming this.

_____

_____

_____

Deborah seemed to miss hearing about the two other gifts J.C. thought were very important. Please make serious study of scripture #66, and ask the Holy Spirit to teach you the important lesson of *how to simply receive*—**just take that with which He has gifted you. It belongs to you!** Study righteousness (right standing with God), scriptures, and *grace (the unlimited, constant favor of God).* Journal what you are learning, and go back at times to look at your journaling to see how much you are growing.

The last thing, and **maybe the most important,** is **the question** Deborah asks at the bottom of page 68 **and J.C.'s answer**.

"When will Holy Spirit come?"

"The moment you ask Him to!"

By doing this, you just made the most important request of your entire life!

Now, thank the Holy Spirit that He is faithful to honor your request.

Chapter 7

HER HOUSE

DEBORAH COULD NOT STOP BEING AMAZED AT the beauty of the house she was seeing. She certainly could not comprehend that *she was* that house with all its glory. J.C. just let Deborah ask all the questions she needed to ask, and He answered her in a way she could not comprehend. She first thought He was teasing, and then, considering the grandeur of the house, she asked if He was being untruthful with her.

1. Why would this be impossible?

2. Have you ever asked Jesus to show *you* as His house?

3. Do you find something interesting in the answer J.C. gave Deborah when she asked if He thought they would be happy in the house? If so, what? Note here.

_____

_____

_____

There is a very spiritual aspect to the seemingly natural outlook Deborah took next as she asked about the cleaning of the house.

4. What spiritual connection do you make between her question about servants and His answer concerning the staff He would give her?

_____

_____

_____

Deborah took a long time looking at the house without a clue that it represented **her**! Spend some time just thinking of yourself as the House of God. Do not let anything **negative** interfere—things like who you were before this moment, unlovely things that have been said about you, failures in your walk with Christ—**nothing negative**. Just see yourself new and beautiful—just like He sees you. Know that the servants He promised Deborah are the servants who will clean (and even now are cleaning) your beautiful house as well.

Look at how J.C. loved the way she was looking at her house He bought for her. At a high cost, He bought *your* house too, and He loves for you to look at yourself with pleasure and joy. If you have been abused and betrayed, this may be hard at first, but spend time each day looking at the heart of Jesus for you and see how much He loves you.

5. Find six scriptures describing the love He has for you, and write them here. Read them daily before you begin your meditation on yourself as His glorious house. It will change your thought process of who you are if you will be diligent to do this *just for you*!

_____

_____

_____

_____

_____

At this moment, you may be like Deborah when she said, "J.C., sometimes you say things that make no sense—at least to me anyway." However, if you will be consistent about daily reading the love-talk of Jesus, He will show you that, in His time "He will get better and better at it!"

To make a confession, I do not like housework; yard work, I tolerate well in spring when it is cool—and I have less and less tolerance for this as the weather gets warmer. So, I can understand Deborah's alarm at realizing she might have to clean this entire house alone.

Often, we enter a relationship with Jesus by promising to clean ourselves up for Him. He, like with Deborah, is trying to say to us, "No, I have a staff for you whose job it is to clean and rearrange your house as you are *able to receive* their expertise and help. I have forgiven you centuries ago, and now what I want from you is to accept MY forgiveness and then **forgive yourself**."

6. What are some things for which you need to forgive yourself?

_____

_____

_____

Your list will probably include some monumental issues with your *real self* and some things will seem less offensive. The reason our list stacks up in categories is because we don't realize that in the eyes of Father, a white lie and a murder are all the same category—which is **missing His best in life for us**.

My list that I made started with events of really bad decisions I made between ages twelve and twenty-seven, and I progressed all the way to forgiving myself for quitting playing the piano and lots of other failures to be my real self. I am learning to forbid the condemnation that comes with dwelling on all of this and to just thank and praise Jesus that He has provided—the payment which allows me to be dressed in His garments of righteousness. I'm learning how to use the staff of helpers He has provided to aid in forgiving myself so I can move onward and upward. Until we know **His love** and **begin to love ourselves**, we are in a war with ourselves and others that we cannot win. This is because **He already has the victor's crown**, and we cannot **take it from** Him, **because** He wants to **give it to us.** (Shout "Hallelujah!" here.)

Read on page 74 how J.C. loved looking at Deborah admiring her new house. That is how He is looking at you and waiting for you begin to see your real house—the one that you **are**.

There is already a twinkle in His eyes as He contemplates the "*more* of you."

Chapter 8

THE SERVANTS

LISTEN AS DEBORAH SPEAKS TO J.C. FIRST THING in the morning. Don't you think she has been up all night deciding her approach to these servants? Can you not see her at the mirror practicing her facial expressions when introduced to her staff? *After all, I* am *the* bride *of a very important person with responsibilities and position to uphold* is probably her thought process.

I think that is funny, and I hope you do as well. It sounds so ridiculous seeing as how the servants are spiritual forces in the kingdom of God *sent by Jesus for the purpose of* delivering, healing, redeeming, and restoring our lives, right?

OK, let's just look at this realistically. Often, once we become Christians, we feel we are in Christ's fish bowl and are being judged by a critical list of dos and don'ts, cans and cannots, shoulds and should nots, rules and regulations, etc. Look at what Christ told Deborah when she was wondering how to behave. On page 77, read His response.

1. List below the things He told her about her servants:

1.

2.

3.

4.

J.C. gave Deborah some time to meditate on His response, and the book tells us why. Write His reason for this below, and know this is how patiently He is dealing with us as we learn who we really are.

_____

_____

_____

When He spoke, He told her (and us) a very important way to get our houses cleaned to perfection by these servants. He said, "*Just learn about them and their jobs,* and in time, you will trust **their judgement.**" Far too often, we are concerned about the judgment of others so strongly that we forget about our servants *and* our Savior! Look at how the fear of judgment stole Deborah's joy and enthusiasm for her day and her house. Trying to judge by other people's standards of a "clean house" will cause us to be unenthusiastic about our lives as the brides of Christ.

At the top of page 78, read how J.C. knows Deborah's struggle, but lets her work through it without interruption. How do you feel about the fact that He is amused?

_____

_____

---

2. At what do you think He is amused about—her struggle? Explain your answer.

_____

_____

_____

Next, we come to the servants' introductions. They are listed below with a scripture alongside. In order to get to know these servants as yours personally, why not find your own scriptures for each of them and use these daily in your life's situations?

Grace—is the enabling power of holy spirits to live godly in Christ. See Luke 2:40. The child in this verse is a child of God. As a child of God, aren't you filled with grace as well?

Righteousness—is the right-standing with God that enables us to "Come boldly to the throne of Grace" (Heb. 4:15-16). It is also a *free gift* (Rom. 5:17)!

Serenity—the dictionary defines serenity as, "the state of being calm, peaceful and untroubled."[2] The Bible says that it is the "Peace of God" that brings this state of mind through Christ Jesus. Hebrews 4:15-16 tells how we arrive there.

Wisdom—the Bible gives great honor to wisdom. See verse #69 in your book to learn the things wisdom will do for you. Note them here and see if they are things from which you can benefit.

Understanding—read verse #68 in your book. It says to get wisdom and learn. Then, comprehend and interpret what you have learned. If in a group, discuss this as to how it relates to life-involvements. For instance, your workplace situations, home life, parenting, friendships, marriage, or other involvement of life.

JOY—I capitalized this one because it is so important for our lives. Without joy, our days are a series of unending fear and dread as we anticipate all the horrible things that could and sometimes do come to us. Read what J.C. wants Deborah to learn about these servants, and find as many scriptures as possible about joy and its effects on the life of a person. Why not make a Joy Journal to refer to at least every other day for Scriptures that will help you or others who are depressed, oppressed, and joyless to become a joyful house? Ask the Holy Spirit to show you the basis for these people's or for your own conditions. Is it a way of finding acceptance, or is it a way to manipulate?

3. What other ways can you think of that people use joylessness and depression?

_____

_____

_____

In these situations, we and everyone who gives in to joylessness and depression are victims. Becoming a joyful house begins with a *choice*!

Self-pity becomes an idol that we bow to in every circumstance, and it demands that others bow as well. God has a plan, see Deuteronomy 30:19. Notice this is not a word just for you, it includes others as well.

Hope—Look at Psalm 42:11. See this verse in light of the above notes on joy. Keep in mind that the soul of man is three parts—mind, will, and emotions. All three must become hopeful in God and not in man or in our own abilities that are apart from His vision for our lives. Read verse #75 in your text. Discuss this if in a group.

Can you hear the poor-old-me mindset through Deborah in last paragraph on page 83? She is ready to give up her beautiful house that J.C. bought for her and is trying to manipulate Him with that pitiful, hopeless statement. Notice how good and upright and unselfish it sounds, but it is against what He has in mind for her. Yes, she has to learn; yes, she has to clean up her act; yes, it will be difficult; but, in the end, she will be the one who wins.

Read the last paragraph on page 84. Always keep in mind that Jesus is pleased with us because He knows that His servants are capable of taking us from the death of fear into life and joy as we learn to follow His plans for who we *really are*!

Chapter 9

A FAMILY REUNION

THIS IS MY FAVORITE CHAPTER IN THE BOOK. IN it, I think Father God points out so many things that we are all guilty of being and doing, yet Jesus is never angry, nor does He change His loving nature because **we fail** to meet the destiny set for us when He chose us as His brides. He knew us before the foundation of the world and thus is not surprised at our actions and reactions because He has a plan outlined in each circumstance to bring us to our position of grace and purpose.

1. Read the first page and give your interpretation of the conversation between Deborah and J.C. Write it here.

_____

_____

_____

Do you think she heard anything He said?

Do you think she was really interested in how her dress made J.C. look to His family? "I don't want to embarrass YOU," she said. His response to this remark shows that, as always, He is aware of what is in our hearts.

_____

_____

_____

2. What do you think her attitude is at this point?

_____

_____

3. Read the paragraph in the middle of page 86. List all the things her mind was thinking about.

_____

_____

_____

Then read verse #76 in the back of the book.

Isn't it interesting that God doesn't participate in that kind of thinking? He will just let us fret and fume and beg Him, and when He doesn't answer us, we become even more fretful and anxious. Why do you think this is true?

_____

_____

_____

It was only when they actually arrived at the event Deborah had been so anxious about that (as J.C. so carefully planned to teach her) she saw why J.C. was not the least bit upset about apparel.

Read scripture #77. It says they "were all clothed in white robes." Do you think Jesus just saw all of

His family clothed in the robes of righteousness He purchased for them by His blood at Calvary? Remember—He looks on the heart and not on the outward appearance. He does not even see diversity-*He made all of us.*

The sentences at the bottom of page 87 and the top of page 88 will help us to gain understanding of how the Father, Jesus, and the Holy Spirit see us on an everyday basis.

4. Find three things in those sentences that tell you about their viewpoint of us, and write them here.

_____

_____

_____

Take a look at the bottom of page 88. Deborah is feeling so close, important, even *proud* to be the bride of J.C. The next moment, she is feeling ignored.

This is what happens when our relationship with Jesus is based on *feelings*. We become subject to being double minded and the promise for this is, "You will be unstable in all your ways" (James 1:6-8 AMP).

How did Deborah try to get her feelings, which were all wrong in the first place, back to her state of mind upon their arrival?

Read the top of page 89, and write your response.

_____

_____

_____

The idea of Christ's bride is one open to lots of interpretation. However, she is of one race, one creed, and for one purpose—*to bring heaven to earth*. That is what Jesus prayed when His followers asked Him to "teach **us** to pray" (Matt. 6:10). Sadly, much of the church today has no concept of how this is done because **our identity**, like Deborah's, is in the image **we can produce**.

It is only as we understand the unity of our own oneness in Christ's mind for His Body that we will see the flesh-man's image begin to take on the image of the Heavenly Man, Jesus.

5. Read 1 Corinthians 15:48-49 to better understand.

(Please read the book's material and the scripture as you consider this carefully and prayerfully. If this is a group study, discuss this image of yourselves after you hear from the Holy Spirit.)

_____

_____

_____

Read the paragraph on page 91 that begins with "righteousness." Consider those with whom you compare yourself and either feel you fall short of or feel you are superior to. Weigh these thoughts in line with the next paragraph, especially the last sentence on bottom of the page and going onto page 92.

Don't you just *love* Deborah's honesty? "That's going to take me a while." Then J.C., who *knew* exactly what her reaction was going to be, shows up.

Can you think of instances when you were being self-centered, and J.C. showed up? Was He angry and condemning? Was He determined to get her to grovel?

Did He just keep asking what she and Righteousness, who refused to accuse her, were talking about? What was His reaction? If you said love, you are right, but what other word can you think of that made this so perfectly demonstrative of Jesus?

_____

_____

_____

He immediately changed the subject from her problem to say, "Let's have fun, Deb. Let's dance!" Suddenly, Deborah could hear the music of heaven. There is always music in heaven. Only when we know how to relax and release ourselves to Him can we begin to *dance through* to the resolution of our self-accusation, condemnation, frustration, and anxiety about who *we* really are and about who *He really is*!

6. Where was the music coming from?

In an orchestra, each instrument has a role to play. It is the same with the bride of Christ. Psalm 139:16-17 says God's eyes saw us before we were formed, so we have a role in our and the world's destiny. Sometimes it's hard to realize this because we are looking at who we are aside from *Him*. However, once we ask Him to redeem our lives from sin's destruction, we are *in Him—never aside from!*

Read the paragraph on page 94 that starts with, "Goodness, no..." Does this make you more determined to get over looking at your shortcomings and nestle closer to Jesus? If not, don't get under condemnation—read on and see how J.C. reacts to Deborah's confusion. If you are in a group, discuss this and, when alone, meditate on His attitude toward *you* as His beloved-His special Golden Girl. Let Him "play the right notes in your ears until your heart can play it back correctly." Then you can be the instrument of His orchestra you were designed to be.

The world is waiting for *everyone* to know that in this place they **are His instrument, have a purpose, and can dance there.**

Chapter 10

I DO VS. I WILL

IF WE WOULD ALL BE TRUTHFUL, WE WOULD ACT *exactly* like Deborah did under these circumstances. We are *so* protective of what is "ours." The truth is that *nothing* is *ours*. It is *all His*! I can hear your mind saying, "But you don't understand. We've worked so hard," or "Our parents left this to us," or "We were here first," and the excuses for our selfishness go on and on. I can say this because I am as guilty of it as anyone reading this—which may be the reason this chapter really gets to me.

In the Bible, read Matthew 5:39-41. Hmm... now read it again. This time prayerfully—like, "Search my heart, Oh God and see if there is any wicked way in me."

1. Write your thoughts or prayer below.

_____

_____

_____

Now, ask the Holy Spirit to show you why we tend to think this way and have so much trouble obeying Jesus's instruction in Matthew 5:39-41. Is it because we **fear lack** more than we **believe God's promises of provision** for us?

_____

_____

_____

Read Psalm 23:1.

God promises that as long we stay in the protection of the Shepherd (hearing His voice and commands), "We shall not lack."

Is this fierce protection of what is "ours" rooted in a **fear of lack**? I am praying about this in my own life, and I have come to realize this particular fear is also deeply rooted in almost everyone.

I will tell you something that happened in my life to prove that we shall not lack. This circumstance helped me learn to let an attitude of lack go.

Several years ago, I was threatened by someone who wanted a parcel of land that belonged to me. I had recently come to understand the power of the spoken Word, and so I determined four things in my heart: one, not to let this cause fear; two, to call forth the truth of God's provision for me; three, to not speak evil of the person who was threatening me; and four, not to take it to man's law, but let the Lord settle it for me.

My husband did not see it that way, so, at times, when I would get settled into a place of peace, he would bring it up and tell me I'd best get a lawyer. I would simple reply, "The Lord will make me the head and not the tail; I will be above only. I will not be beneath, because I will obey the commands of the Lord." This was my prayer from Deuteronomy 28:13.

Now keep in mind that I was just a "child" in standing on God's Word, but the Holy Spirit was teaching me, and He enabled me to hold fast. The threat of a trial went on for months. Finally, it was resolved, and I was ruled as "the head and not the tail" (Deut. 28:13 KJV). Even with this experience, I still have to be very mindful of every detail in situations the enemy creates as an opportunity for me to fear lack.

**See note at end of this lesson.

How do you interpret J.C.'s question to Deborah on page ninety-eight about *laws and covenants*?

_____

_____

_____

2. Why did He question her wanting to debate Him about this? Write your thoughts here.

_____

_____

_____

As you read on into the bottom of page 99, can you identify with the way Deborah is approaching J.C.? How often we argue with the plans He has for us and then vacillate concerning our or His decision.

_____

_____

_____

At the bottom page 99, J.C. reminds Deborah that she cannot have it both ways.

3. Are there situations in your life in which you are trying to have something both ways? Are you seeing one thing in the Bible or hearing something from the Holy Spirit that you _know_ is the "Path of Life," yet your flesh just cannot get there?

If you have ever reached, or are now at, that point, note it here.

_____

_____

_____

Notice how J.C., **without condemnation**, gives Deborah space to get to the truth of who she really is. He just guides her to truth and then confirms it.

So, don't beat yourself up in these situations, but learn from them how to communicate with the Christ in you, so you may unlock any areas where you are locked into a pattern of unhealthy behavior and/or understanding.

This chapter is so funny to me. Probably because in many situations we react just like Deborah. Mind you, we are not always as honest as Deborah. As a matter of fact, when I hear His instructions, I often say, "Oh yes, I know that." He doesn't say, "Liar, liar, pants on fire." He just gives time for insight through experience, prayer, and submission—like being honest about my feelings and opening my heart to understand and commit to doing things *His way* in spite of the desires of my flesh and the advice of the world. Read on page 101 how J.C. tells Deborah about the Spirit of His Dad's corporation.

Can't you feel for Deborah in the next paragraph (page 102)? J.C. has just explained the mind-set of a victor versus the mind-set of a loser. Now, J.C. continues to tell Deborah that when we operate in anything other than the kind of kingdom victory that profits our **souls**, we lose regardless of the world's ruling. J.C. has just closed the door to argument with truth—that's how the P.R. person of the kingdom operates *–His truth will silence offense.*

Remember, **offense always builds a fence around us!**

Read the paragraph at the bottom of page 103 and the top of 104 and be encouraged that you are not a quitter, and you **will win** the battle to find who you **really are** and **were meant to be** from the beginning of time.

NOTE: I do not like telling this sort of thing because I do not want anyone to think this is the only plan for every situation. God can use any number of methods to gain victory for us. In this instance, this is what I believed I was instructed to do. The keys are **hearing Him and **obeying** whatever is **His plan**. That was what I did in this case. On many other occasions, I have had to learn the hard way.

Chapter 11

H.S. IS TO LIVE WHERE?

PRECIOUS, CARNAL DEB! LIKE US, SHE IS STILL thinking and asking for lesser things without an understanding of how little value they have in the much larger scheme of her life.

Precious J.C. with His invaluable sense of loving humor at her (and our) ignorance of the grand scheme prepared for us before the foundation of the world in Him. He laughs at her foolishness as He presents the priceless gift of H.S.'s presence in her house to bring sparkle to her **entire** life as opposed to each moment singularly. Two questions here:

1. In the sense of allegory, what does Deborah's house represent?

_____

_____

_____

2. At top of page 106, read the paragraph. What does Deborah's reaction indicate to you? Relate to both her questions and give **your** answers here.

_____

_____

_____

At the bottom of page 106, read the last sentence and reflect on the difference in Deborah's reaction here and the reactions in Chapter 10. She seems to be "growing in grace and in the nurture and admonition of the Lord." It is only as we learn to see Jesus as a **nurturer** that we can relax in circumstances that are beyond our comprehension.

At the top of page 107 is a lesson we all need to learn as ones seeking to grow into followers of our *real* path in life. Most of us have never understood what that path is, and those of us who have thought we did have often tried to make a plan to carry it out.

Making a plan isn't a bad thing, but following the way of a **perfectly outlined plan** is so much better. **The Holy Spirit has that plan for each life that ever came into being.** That is so hard to fathom and explains why we need His presence and His teachings to show us how much bigger *we are than simply us!*

Look at how J.C. describes the job of Holy Spirit! He is an *interior designer!* He will change us from the inside out. This is the opposite of the world's understanding of personal change. He will show us *who we are,* and then, by looking at **that person**, we can become who we are **designed** to be. **More success is found in a peaceful co-existence with our own person than with the accolades of the crowd**. We have to learn how to know the Designer in a way that leads us to live *above needing* the praises of people and know how to live out from **who we are in Christ**.

At the bottom of 107, we see the former Deb appearing once again. This time, she is being defensive of her position—an indication of her need for the Holy Spirit. Her personal interior décor needs refurbishing, and, try as she might, **she** just can't get it done.

At the same time, she is fearful of the coming of the Holy Spirit and the changes He will make to her **comfortable** state of existence in Christ. She is even afraid of what other people will think when H.S. comes to live in her house.

Have you ever been in this place personally or in a group or in a relationship with an individual who had Deborah's anxieties about the Holy Spirit? **If so, with the Holy Spirit's help,** examine your thoughts and feelings and opinions in the light of the remainder of the book.

Read at the bottom of page 108 and the top of 109 to see how J.C. handled her reaction. **Jesus**

just never forces His way into our lives any deeper than we want to go. He simply leaves us to our own plans until we get so miserable with trying to set our lives right that we *ask* to be shown *His way*. It is so sad to see and be people who have so much potential but **just settle for hope for better.** *This* **is the world's way of trying to satisfy the hunger on the *inside* of us with *external* things and substances.** It's akin to using a Band-Aid to cover a six-inch gash—the bleeding simply will not stop.

3. Who appears to Deborah in her time of broken-ness and unwillingness to accept H.S.?

_____

_____

_____

Isn't that so like Jesus? He extended His grace, which is the *favor and empowerment* to *accept* deeper things in order to *become* our higher selves. Grace simply *announces* the visitor and gives her a tissue.

Do you think Grace is saying, "Get up, Dear, you're not a baby any longer"?

4. Consider what Deborah is continuing to fear? Read the last sentence at the bottom of page 109 and answer that question here. Discuss this if in a group.

_____

_____

_____

5. As far as the Holy Spirit is concerned, do you identify with this fear?

_____

_____

_____

On page 110, notice Deborah's reaction to Righteousness.

6. In the first paragraph at the top of page 111, Grace mentions two ways people consider the gift of righteousness. Which of these is your concept? Answer here.

_____

_____

_____

Discuss your answer if this is a group study. If this is a personal study, prayerfully ask for understanding as this is very necessary in order to progress in becoming Christ-like.

7. Read Romans 5:16-17 to help instill this understanding in your heart. If you are floundering a bit, read the two things Grace asked as she prayed for Deborah. **Then, ask for them.**

Righteousness will show us the things that are negatively affecting our relationship with Jesus. Take note below.

_____

_____

_____

8. At the top of page 112, what things did Righteousness point out as her problems that kept Deborah from being able to be her real self? Then, notice how He covers this revelation with love. **"Perfect love will cast out your fear"**

(1 John 4:18 KJV) of both the Holy Spirit and people.

From the middle of pages 112 and 113 until "you have begun so beautifully," there are six things Righteousness points out that the Holy Spirit wants to give to each of us.

9. Find and list those six things here. There are many, many more that can be found and lived out from in His Promise Book!

_____

_____

_____

_____

_____

_____

Read these items over and over, accept them *as you*, and hear Jesus and yourself chuckle!

Chapter 12

FOR ALL MEN

WHEN MY FRIENDS AND I WERE YOUNG, WE would say to each other, "First you say you will, and then you won't. Then you say you do, and then you don't." It seems Deborah thought J.C. was that kind of person. This is not unusual—all of us at times feel like this about heavenly things.

For instance, read Luke 24:36-44 and notice the disciples' shock, doubt, and need to actually touch Jesus, all mixed with joy and excitement. All this took place in the space of minutes. Jesus did not get angry, because He already knew what was going to happen when He appeared to them. In essence, paraphrasing the words in verse #44, He said, "I told you I would be back, why are you so shocked?" Why do you think they were shocked?

Maybe all the events they **had just *seen* caused them to forget His *promise*.**

Relate this to Deborah's reactions at the bottom of pg. 115 and first paragraph on 116. Write your answer here, and discuss if in a group.

_____

_____

_____

Note how many times she asked instead of trusting that it would all work out for her good, and before you judge *her*, remember the last situation in which the outcome was unknown to you! How many times did you question God about what was going on?

_____

_____

_____

I am smiling here as I know how many times I've asked for information of the outcome in *my* circumstances. For instance, recently I went to the beach for a week without the suitcase that had my clothes and bathing suits in it. My first reaction was to scream. I controlled that urge with the Lord's help and began to listen to His voice. All I heard was, "This *has* to work for your good, because I have promised it." All afternoon in my traveling clothes, I kept smiling and saying, "Thank You, Lord, that this is working for my good." Of course, my enemy was saying, "Well you're not out there on the beach, are you? Is this *good*?" Late that night, as I was still struggling to settle my thoughts and go to sleep, I heard "Didn't you write the *Bride of Christ Book* and aren't you My bride?"

I said, "Yes Lord, I am Your bride."

Then I heard, "Go to sleep because tomorrow, we're going on a shopping whirl." Do you think I was smiling then?

If you want to note some particularly *trying* incident of your own, do so here. Share, if you choose,
in a group session.

_____

_____

_____

On page 116 at the bottom, notice J.C.'s reply
to Deborah.

1. Can you get a sense for what He means by His
answer to her praises? Write your answer here.

_____

_____

_____

If you ever doubt that Jesus has a sense of
humor, note the only part of Deborah's outfit He
suggested.

2. Name that part of her outfit here.

_____

Try to relate to what Deborah was seeing at the bottom of page 118 and the top of 119. I have not personally had much exposure to that kind of neighborhood, so I cannot say that I would not feel unsafe.

3. Answer below, would you have left the safety of the car with J.C.? Now, before you write, "Well sure, with Jesus I would have been safe." Yes, we've all heard Jesus promise that He will never leave us and that He lives in us. This along with, go into *all* the world—not just where we know the patterns and feel safe! Hearing and doing are two different things, and I think all of us would have had some trepidation about climbing out of the car.

_____

_____

_____

4. Another question: Why did Deborah think **H.S. would disagree with J.C.?** Don't judge her, however, as often we hear J.C. asking us to go into a situation or behave differently in a current situation, and we say, "I just don't believe the Holy Spirit would tell me to do that." Or, every time we *do* hear Him, we keep saying, "Is that really You, God?" Write your thoughts on the question here, please.

_____

_____

_____

How long has it been since Jesus took you on an adventure you could not grasp from **His** perspective—as a **Royal Event**? Deborah thought she had on her best outfit.

5. Read Zechariah 3:1-5, and notice the following three things.

1. Who accuses Joshua about his clothing being dirty?

2. What two things does the Lord take from Joshua?

3. In verse 5, who asked for Joshua to be clothed with "a crown and clean clothes"? This sounds like a considerably Royal Event. One at which, in the book's following paragraphs, we see Jesus reigning in humility and compassion—His nature that Deborah (and we) must learn in order to reign with Him.

Deborah keeps referring to "**these people**" as if they aren't known by God just the same as she is. Then when she brings up being "exposed" to them to H.S.–once again expecting Him to disagree with J.C.—He said what we should **all** come to understand. Read the bottom of page 121 and the first two paragraphs of page 122, and let the things Holy Spirit wants Deborah to understand sink into your realization and write them here.

_____

_____

6. Think of a situation in which you have said judgmental things about someone—like Deborah's reply to H.S. If you feel comfortable doing so, write it here.

_____

_____

_____

H.S. never replied to her ugliness. The Holy Spirit is like that—gentle, kind, longsuffering. What amazing, life-changing advice did He give Deborah?

_____

_____

_____

As you read this chapter, note how Deborah continues to say (in effect), "Yes, but..." The fact that she is simply defending her refusal to obey J.C.'s plan is obvious to everyone but her.

Is there a current situation or a past one that this attitude calls to mind? If so, try to see the persons or the situation from the perspective that He means **all things for good for His children and, on the cross, He bought all of us as His own**. Notice that on page 124 J.C. is enjoying the people on the street.

7. Can you envision this, or do you agree with Deborah? If you truthfully agree with Deborah, read and answer the questions on page 125, then reflect on your answers and read the page again. Now, read J.C.'s thoughts on the bottom of the page and just know you are loved and can learn through the Holy Spirit's teachings.

Chapter 13

REAL PEOPLE

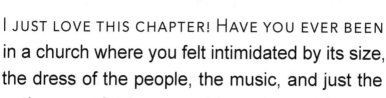

I JUST LOVE THIS CHAPTER! HAVE YOU EVER BEEN in a church where you felt intimidated by its size, the dress of the people, the music, and just the entire event? I have, and I must say, I have a lot of respect for Deborah's excitement. I wasn't excited a bit!

Do you have a special seat at your church? I do, and I have a plethora of excuses about it—my legs are long, I hear well there, and so on. **The truth is I like sitting there and want that seat.** Now, mind you, I smile and don't make a fuss when someone else is there when I arrive, but I certainly try to get there first.

J.C. knows my heart just as He knew the hearts of those at the church they were attending and Deborah's when she was "leaving her Bible" at her church. It's called wanting the best place for ourselves regardless of others. Isn't it interesting that this is all done in the *sanctuary*?

On the top of page 129, read J.C.'s comment on Deborah's assessment of that seemingly universal need.

In the remainder of the events during the service, *try to see yourself as Deborah,* new to all of this formality, grandeur, music, and solemnity— all of it!

1. Would you have felt free to cry, to sing with all robust joy, to say amen, or to encourage the pastor?

2. Do you wonder why she did not catch on to the apparent rules for proper behavior sooner?

3. Why do you think J.C. would not look at her?

All of these questions may be viewed and answered differently at different moments of consideration but will require *gut-wrenching honesty* in order to hear truth and possibly be set free in areas. If in a group, this makes for interesting discussion.

Next, go back to their arrival at the church and see yourself as one of the members of the church who are familiar with the order of service. Try to put yourself in their place.

4. Would you think it strange that she was crying?

5. Would you stare at her for singing with such joy, or maybe snicker with your friends?

6. When she said "Amen," would you have turned and stared to express your disdain?

7. Would you have smiled politely from a distance or spoken kindly to them as they left?

Now, before going further, look at all of your answers, and again, putting yourself into each situation, try to decide **what in you** triggered each of your responses.

Next, we find Deborah in the car accusing J.C. Isn't it always easier to blame someone *else* than to be honest with ourselves? Blaming instead of owning the deep-seated, hidden things in us that are causing us problems at work, at home, at church, and socially can still be working against us.

Notice, J.C. did not respond to accusations—a good note-to-self.

Then Holy Spirit, in His always gentle, loving way of teaching us, leaned over and brushed off her suit.

8. Why do you think He did this particular thing at this particular moment?

_____

_____

_____

Perhaps it was to reinforce what J.C. said to her at the top of the second paragraph on page 134.

9. Do you have an opinion about that statement?

_____

_____

_____

10. In the last sentence on page 134 and the first paragraph on page 135, Jesus gives us four ways that we miss living in the abundance of who

we really are. List those here, and reflect on them in your own life.

_____

_____

_____

Isn't it great when we come to understand that Father, Son, and Holy Ghost have wonderful senses of humor? Refer to the bottom of page 135. **We are, after all made in their image.**

Deborah's saying, "I'm sorry," is an example of how repentance can help us to live free of much that would bind us to self-degradation.

Chapter 14

"Living Rooms"

WELL, ALL OF A SUDDEN, WE FIND A NEW Deborah! She is contemplating *her* lack of understanding of J.C. instead of *his* lack of understanding her. This leads her to think about her relationship with Righteousness. She becomes aware, with the help of the Holy Spirit, of all her striving to *act* like Righteousness when all the time simply *being* like him was a matter of opening Jesus's gift of Him (read scripture #10 in back of the book) and learning to *recieve* who He is as our gift.

What do people who give us gifts hope we will do with them? If your answer is "open them, use them, and enjoy them," then you know why Jesus went through all the pain and shame of the cross to give us grace and the free gift of righteousness.

1. Can you relate to the Holy Spirit as an interior designer? How about as a partner in their company? Express your thoughts and feelings here.

_____

_____

_____

At the bottom of page 140 and the top of page 141, there are some other ways for you to think of the Holy Spirit. The last sentence gives the way He thinks of Himself for you. Is it easier to think of Him in that way for you?

_____

_____

_____

2. Why do you think that the cleaning of Deborah's house is always referred to as cleaning the upstairs?

_____

_____

_____

Oh my! Does dread live in your "upstairs"? It has certainly lived in mine. I remember as a girl hearing my mother say, "You know someone told me, 'Miss Bess, you dread your work. Quit dreading it, and you can get it done.'" These "upstairs antiques" can often be traced to family traits that have been instilled in us as children either by word or deed or both. The Holy Spirit is ready to take this and other things before the Righteous Judge. By confessing and repenting (which incidentally, means "a change of mind"), they can be covered by the testimony of Jesus's Blood at the cross and cleaned out of our lives.

Notice another negative characteristic in the middle paragraph of page 142. What crippling force in her life does Deborah attribute to dread?

_____

_____

_____

At the bottom of page 142, look at how "the accuser of the brethren" begins to speak to Deborah's heart and mind to stop her progress.

3. What fear, that we have already seen, does he use to try to discourage her getting rid of dread and inadequacy?

The way H.S. speaks to her fear and dread along with what others may think of her in the middle of page 143 inspires each of us to understand Him and His nature more fully.

Just keep this in mind, He tells her **He** will not judge her. How often do we judge **ourselves** negatively and accredit those thoughts to H.S., when, all the while, it's the accuser trying to keep us in bondage?

John 3:17 says, "For God did not send His Son into the world to condemn the world, but that the world might be saved through Him." The Holy Spirit is trying to help us find the "treasures" of more heavenly places in us. What are some of your heavenly treasures you know the two of you will find as you clean your upstairs? List them here.

_____

_____

_____

For insight, use the paragraph at the bottom of page 143 as you clean your "upstairs." It will help you know when you are at the correct door, and show you what is in each room. List some of the things you're working on here, if you choose.

_____

_____

_____

4. Write in all caps the only thing the Holy Spirit needs to have from us to enter and clean up our upstairs.

_____

_____

_____

5. Write here and remember what, on page 144, H.S. told Deborah is "the lie."

6. What are the three big "piles" H.S. tells Deborah that He sees in Dread's chain links?

List them here, and meditate to see what the Holy Spirit says to you.

1.

2.

3.

7. Now take each one and write what indicates its presence and then the solution to its destructive force.

_____

_____

_____

**Be certain you read far enough to find the first plateau of forgiveness and then continue by answering here. Do not take this lightly as it is the key to the other doors.

_____

_____

_____

_____

_____

Look who has shown up to help Holy Spirit and Deborah clean. Also, note that they are totally unperturbed by the piles of spiritual debris. They know their job.

Watch as Grace floods the area with light in order to better see what needs help.

Titus 2:11 (AMPC) says: "For the Grace of God (His unmerited favor and blessing) has come forward (appeared) for the deliverance from sin and the eternal salvation for all mankind." Grace always brings light to any subject.

Please be aware that the process isn't always finished in a day or a week. The Holy Spirit will take as long as He and the other helpers of His nature need to finish their job perfectly. Our job is to give the key of permission to Him and let Him do His work in the way necessary to deliver and save us from us.

H.S. and the others finally got to the bottom of the pile and showed Deborah the root problem—one that all of us experience and can identify with, but must eliminate. Back on page 150, what does H.S. tell Deborah the name of this force is? How does He say it hides from our sight? What is the false goal it shows us? What is the goal that we are seeking?

_____

_____

_____

The force that becomes our motivator is _____! In its presence, what disappears?

_____

Do you feel loved by Jesus? If not, ask the Holy Spirit to come into your heart and begin to show you how loved you really are. Often our past experiences are more real to us than the truth of how Jesus sees us. Experiences into which Holy Spirit is ready and waiting for an invitation to come in, change our perspectives, and decorate our spiritual house. Remember, you have the key of permission for Him to do this, and He *loves* His job because He *loves us*! "He has stayed with projects much larger and more tedious that yours," so learn to use His skills and enjoy Him.

_____

_____

_____

_____

_____

Chapter 15

THE MYSTERY REVEALED

THIS CHAPTER IS AN EXAMPLE OF HOW PEOPLE whose only example of fathering has been an absentee father or a poor reflection of his position in the home. When this happens, the concept of Father God becomes somewhat negative. As you may remember from the first chapter, Deborah's father-experience left a lot to be desired. Hence, her apprehensive thoughts and questions to J.C.

On page 155, J.C. assures Deborah of His Father's love for her as His bride. J.C. also tells her about the things that the Father wants to give her. Deborah asked J.C. a question that we sometimes find ourselves asking Jesus. What was Jesus's answer to her question? This is the answer to *all* our questions. Write it here.

_____

_____

_____

Our relationship with Jesus, the Holy Spirit, and the Father is all about how **we** identity with **them**. They decided before the world began how **they** wanted to identify with **us**. Below, honestly try to express how you identify with each of these parts of the Godhead. Remember, *there are no wrong answers, just honest ones.* So, write what you see as how you identify with each, and, in a month or a year, come back and see if, like Deborah, that identification has changed. Write your answers here.

_____

_____

_____

_____

Now, at the top of page 156, see how J.C. led Deborah to think about her heart (or her identity) with the Father. Perhaps, instead of two hearts, there are actually three: Should be, could be, or As He Is.

It is all a matter of understanding that our heart isn't based on behavior. Instead, it is an *identity* issue. The Word says that "We are raised up with Christ; and seated with Him in the heavenly realms in Christ Jesus, in order that in the coming ages, He might **show (us)** the incomparable riches of His Grace, expressed in His kindness to us in Christ Jesus" (Eph. 2:6-7 NIV, addition mine).

So, how would we act and think differently if we began to see ourselves **already** seated in Heavenly places, with an **invitation** to, "Come **boldly** to the **throne of Grace** that we may obtain mercy and **find grace to help** in time of need" (Heb. 4:16 KJV, emphasis mine)?

_____

What does "Come boldly to the throne of Grace" mean to you?

_____

_____

_____

Let's look at translations of these words in the Strong's New Exhaustive Concordance of the Bible. In the original language the word "boldly" means, "all outspokenness, frankness, assurance."[3] The word "throne" is translated from the word "power."[4] The word "grace" is translated "the divine influence upon the heart, and its reflection in the life."[5]

Make a sentence that says what these translated words mean to you. If you are confused, ask the Holy Spirit to help you to understand.

_____

_____

Let me tell you a personal example of coming boldly to the throne of grace and finding help in time of need. I started smoking very early in my childhood. By the time I was thirty-five, I had been inhaling cigarette smoke for twenty-five years. I could not breathe lying down on my pillow at night—I had to prop up to sleep. I quit once for three years and started back (something I think many addicts fight).

Finally, one morning early, I laid down on the floor in surrender and said to God, "God, if You don't want me to meet You one day with a cigarette in my hand, *you* are going to have to do something. I have done everything I know to do to quit this harming of Your temple."

Why did I tell you that? To show you how we can come with all outspokenness, frankly, with assurance to the power of the divine influence upon the **heart** and (see) its reflection on our life. I quit very quickly after that and never looked back.

What had happened? **My identity changed. In my heart, I no longer saw myself as a smoker.** I saw myself as a free person. **I had a different heart.** I could come to Father with great joy and thanksgiving for my freedom that *He* had given me.

See yourself as it speaks about on page 157 in the first paragraph. Begin to view yourself as **"a part of Jesus"** and realize that **You bring** the **Father such joy**! If you will keep this in mind before you begin to worship and pray, you will begin visit the throne room more often. **Worship and prayer will become an opportunity, not an obligation.**

Can you believe the Father has a plan for your part in His kingdom? Most of us are much greater than we ever imagined. **Be bold—ask Him! Knock, and He will open doors for you. Seek, and you will find your kingdom place.**

1. When you see His vision, write it here.

_____

_____

Now, begin through the power of grace to step into all that the Father has always known you to be. **Be bold**—it's your gift and "the gifts and calling of God are without repentance" (Rom. 11:29 KJV).

On page 160, the people God sent to her were not too keen on Deborah! Has God ever had you witness to someone who was not too keen on you? Have you or anyone you were witnessing to ever questioned that God would *talk* to you? Have you or do you question that God talks to people? Write how you feel about these questions here.

_____

_____

_____

_____

Read at the bottom of 160 how God handles all of these things. When *we* are secure in **our**

place in His kingdom and in His love, we can change other's hearts by the power of that love. Read the gifts of His Spirit again (Gal. 5:22-23). Each gift *builds* on the other one, and the Bible says, "Against such things there is no law" (Gal. 5:23 KJV).

Read page 163 through 164 beginning with, "In the years to come…" Ask the Holy Spirit to give you a revelation of what the Father is saying to your heart about *who you really are* in the eyes of Father God.

It is my sincere hope you are now (and will continue to be) more seriously contented in how very loved you are by Jesus, the Holy Spirit, and the Father. If so, this book has done what the Father intended.

NOTES

1. LEXICO.COM #1.1, #1.2

2. "Serenity." The Merriam-Webster.
com Dictionary, Merriam-Webster Inc.,
https//www.merriam-webster/serenity.

3. "Boldly" Strong, James Exhaustive
Concordance of the Bible, Thomas Nelson
Publishers 1984 #3954, p. 137

4. ibid. #2362 p. 1097

5. ibid. #5485 p. 431

CPSIA information can be obtained
at www.ICGtesting.com
Printed in the USA
FSHW021510100520
69895FS